SACRED SECRETS OF ESOTERIC CHRISTIANITY

By Louis Sefer

Copyright © 2023

Table of Contents

Exploring Esoteric Christianity

Esotericism

There is more to Truth and Reality than what most minds wish to imagine and consider. It frequently appears to be more appealing to sit in the dark where we cannot see anything than to face the dazzling brightness. Isn't the blindness in both cases the same? The former is blissful ignorance, whereas the latter is an initial jolt that eventually brings peace to the soul. It is the brave person who seeks Truth, no matter how unpleasant or shocking it may be.

We do not claim to represent Truth in this text; rather, we provide routes to it. Because there are different types of individuals who seek Truth, humanity can be divided into two groups:

1) "The Many," the believers, those who are loyal and content with the dogmas of their creed and resistant to any doctrines that contradict and upset their beliefs and faith, especially the higher revelations of the Paraclete, or thc Holy Spirit.

2) "The Few," the seekers, those who have become disillusioned with irrational faiths and creeds that do not satisfy the intellect or the evolving conscicnce of the inner self, and who seek spiritual knowledge and experience to fill the empty heart of spiritual desire.

Martinism's co-founder, St. Martin, refers to this second group as "Men of Desire."

Recognizing this difference within humanity since the dawn of time, the higher intelligences in charge of man's progress founded religions with dual divisions that catered to the two types of men.

Martinism's spiritual guardians, the "Minor Spirits," have realized that the masses of man are still too puerile to participate in their own salvation and the unfoldment of their divinity. Only a few were capable of doing so.

Religion, then, has its mysteries, an esoteric side to its nature, established to nurture and nourish those few who were qualified to receive the higher teachings that would stimulate the awakening and unfoldment of their divine consciousness, their seed potential of Christhood or Buddhahood, and establish them firmly on the path of discipleship, that they may become Holy Spirit initiates.

"But we speak the wisdom of God in a mystery, even the hidden wisdom, which God ordained before the world unto our glory." (1Cor 2:7)

Religion, in order to be valuable, must reach the hearts of mankind at various stages of evolution, as shown in the symbolism of Jacob's dream.

Its ideas and precepts should comprise both basic and higher teachings of Cosmic principles to help man fulfill the ancient threefold commandment:

"Know thyself, know thyself as God, and know they enemy."

·Esoteric teachings are those that are only revealed to a select few. St. Paul referred to such manna as "meat," as opposed to "milk" fit for the many—or "babes"—those whose soul-experience, personal progress, and consciousness are still at the basic level.

Origen, one of the early Fathers of Christianity, taught that the esoteric side, or secret mysteries, would be disclosed only after the members of the church's congregation stopped doing evil.

Sinners were admonished not to sin, but despite the simplicity of this command, the early Christian community found it difficult to put these teachings into reality, and earnest seekers became scarce as a result.

The "straight and narrow gate" entrance was gradually closed and withdrawn from the Christian institution, and its presence was forgotten by lay members and priestly alike.

The "keys" to the Kingdom of Heaven were no longer in the hands of the Apostle Peter's successors—the exact nature of these "keys" is unknown to the vast majority of religious representatives of God, much less the lay follower. The latter is unaware of its existence.

Nowadays, blind leaders deceive their equally blind followers into believing in salvation based on a faulty reading of the scriptures. However, this circumstance has always occurred in religious instruction temples in the past. The Master Jesus was outspoken about these misguided teachers of Spiritual Law.

Religion's initial aim was to deliver the Secret Wisdom of the Ages to man's minds and hearts at a certain stage in his mental and spiritual growth.

Humanity is required to be accountable for their own salvation and liberation from matter's bonds. Because man is expanding and progressing toward the Light, revelation would have to be continual to satisfy man's unceasing inquiry, growing knowledge, and comprehension of the Nature of Being, his Soul's ontology. Resistance to future "Comforter" disclosures is an act of fanaticism that causes the resistant one's evolutionary desire to halt and prolong the sleep of consciousness in the tomb of matter.

The conflict between gnosis, the Ancient Wisdom, and progressive revelation drove the esoteric side of religions, particularly Christianity, to withdraw formally from the outer, exoteric effort and form secret organizations and Orders, keeping the secret teachings in their archives.

Religion's esoteric side is what breathes vitality into the institution as a whole. Without the mystical component, religion becomes a farce, a hoax, and a breeding ground for corruption. Dogmas and foundationless ideas and faiths merely insult human intelligence, resulting in the rebellion of the human soul striving for knowledge.

Prophets and sages, exponents of gnosis, established religions and organizations with the purpose of guiding the masses many steps closer to the Light. They also hinted at an advanced way that would hasten the spiritual development of individuals who choose to follow such a path.

The "strait and narrow gate" was offered by the Master Jesus. Jeremiah, acting as Omniety's scribe and spokesperson, proposed that people *"... inquire about the ancient paths (Jer 6:16) "*

Many stories in the scriptures serve as manuals for practical spiritual practices of development. For example, there is Jacob's Ladder; Elijah's Mount experience; the different stages of Moses' experiences with Divinity; Ezekiel's Merkabah or sky-chariot; Jesus' 40-day fast on the Mount with Satan; events in Jesus' life, and so on.

Many of Christianity's doctrines, rites, tenets, and ideas are derived from ancient religions and Mystery Schools. This fact can be discovered through comparative religions research.

The doctrines of heaven and hell, the last judgment, the mediation of the Logos on behalf of humanity's salvation, and the Eucharist, for example, all have counterparts in the cults of Mithras, Zoroastrianism, and the Essenes.

It is also in the realm of possibility that the enlightened minds of religion's forefathers were enlightened with the same illumination of the Spirit regarding Cosmic rules of the universe that guides every spark of God. This would explain the striking parallels between religions.

Truth, since it is One, is eternal and immovable. The manner in which Truth is communicated varies from culture to culture and from age to age, yet its essential character remains constant.

Religious founders were and continue to be exceptional individuals from the perspective of an uneducated mankind. Each and every enlightened-one, on the other hand, teaches of the possibility of man attaining the same degree of almighty godhood by realizing his spiritual potential and emulating the great ones who incarnate to demonstrate the Way, to Moksha, to Freedom.

Parts of the Ancient Wisdom, or the gnosis of the Bodhisattvas, were preserved in ancient scriptures such as the Avesta, Vedas, Tao Teh Ching, Book of Dzan, Psalms, Ecclesiastes, and many other apocryphal writings. Certain portions of the Ancient Wisdom, such as the Qabalah of Judaism, were passed down verbally from Master to chela.

Esoteric Christianity is the gnosis given by Master Jesus to an inner circle of students, as a practical collective-stream correlating to bhakti, raja, jnana, kundalini, laya, and karma yoga. Its theories and principles are founded on Ancient Wisdom. However, for the disciples of the new dispensation, the Piscean and Aquarian Ages, Jesus revealed more advanced features of the gnosis. Even to his most devoted disciples, he declared that there were higher truths that they were not yet prepared to receive:

"I have many things to say to you, but ye cannot bear them now." (John 16:12)

In this passage, Jesus alluded to the continuation of revelation and promised that higher teachings will be provided at the appropriate time. *"Are current Christian adherents absorbing these lessons in this age?"* one might ask. Is it possible to learn more about the nature of these teachings?

There was a long-held notion in the early days of the Church that Jesus stayed with his followers for a long time after his ascension in order to teach them more about the gnosis.

According to the gnostic literature "Pistis Sophia," Jesus remained with his followers for eleven years following his resurrection.

St. Iraneus, bishop of Lyons, agreed with this view, despite his opposition to most, if not all, other gnostic teachings. He claimed in his book "Against Heresies" that the Apostles themselves testified that Jesus lived to a ripe old age.

In light of this, one wonders about the allegation that Jesus' grave is in Srinagar, India, as mentioned by locals living in the area.

According to a current Esoteric Christian school, the gnosis passed down from Initiator to candidate was separated into two parts:

1) The Purifying Mysteries--For the sinner who seeks to be cleansed of karmic inclinations and stains.

2) The Illuminating Mysteries--for those who want to study and comprehend

reality and Maya, the microcosm and macrocosm, and so on.

Spiritual gnosis initiates are the mythical Peters who guard Heaven's pearly gates. They possess the keys to illumination, understanding, and the principles that would enable the applicant to enter Heaven, the Kingdom of God within his consciousness— exactly where Jesus predicted it would be— within oneself, rather than in the afterlife or in some physical location on Earth. His parables are sufficient to persuade one of this.

Certain Church Fathers, including Origen, Clement of Alexandria, and Ignatius, mentioned the existence of esoteric doctrines within early Christianity. They admired the esoteric teachings and would have shouted them from the rooftops if it hadn't been for the dumb brains of worldly men, some of whom were dressed in priestly robes.

This was done by Origen, who was afterwards anathemized by Emperor Justinius, who presided over the Fifth Ecumenical Council in 553 AD. Many of Origen's works were set on fire. We have discussed how the gnosis was removed from public view.

Throughout the ages, various church councils replaced the gnosis with impious creeds and dogmas that no longer mirrored Jesus' original teachings.

Some esotericists believe that Joseph of Arimathea was the protector of the esoteric church of Christianity, much as "Peter" was seen to be the leader of the earthly church. The secret church was known as the "Secret Church of the Holy Grail." According to legend, Joseph, a hidden disciple of Jesus, traveled to Glastonbury, England, bringing with him relics reputed to be infused with divine virtue.

The grail, the chalice used by Jesus during the "Last Supper," and the spear that wounded him while he was hanging on the cross were among these relics. The Grail vanished from the physical world due to corruption within the church in subsequent years. King Arthur and Merlin founded the Order of the Knights of the Round Table to pursue the Holy Grail.

In reality, the search most likely took place within the Soul, as the Grail represents a spiritual aspect in man's being. Only the pure are supposed to be able to perceive God.

According to one version of the Grail legend, Sir Galahad, the youthful Knight who discovered the Grail, represented man's refined essence. Only in this cleansed state is it possible for man to "see" God—and live—but not as an average mortal, because the lesser components of his nature would have "perished" in God's consuming, transmuting flame.

Gnosticism

The Order of the Grail was not the only Esoteric Christian sect. Gnostics claim that they, too, were bestowed the secret teachings of Jesus through a "Doctrine of the Heart," which was passed down to them by lesser-known apostles like Thomas and Mark.

Gnostics saw Peter as representing the esoteric side of Christianity. Some Gnostics believe that Simon Magus founded Gnosticism. Nothing is known about this strange personality save that he clashed with Peter in a psychic war in Acts and was defeated. Many people feel that this myth was made up by exoteric Christian priests in order to discredit Gnosticism as a whole.

Gnosis, from which the word Gnosticism is derived, originates from the Greek word "Gnostikos," which signifies one who has knowledge. Bishop John Bricaud defines it as follows in his book Esoteric Christian Doctrine:

"The greatest religious science, which is accurate understanding of the three worlds, divine, spiritual, and material, and their interrelationship."

Gnosticism teaches students secret methods of investigation and access into the inner depths of the soul. Beliefs and sheer faith were not encouraged in the Gnostic Masters' teachings.

As previously stated, St. Iraneus condemned Gnostics for their mystical beliefs. He condemned their spiritual literary creations, their gospels, as blasphemous. It is clear why Iraneus was opposed to their teachings. Gnosticism provided searchers with direct access to Omniety, undermining the priesthood's status as the alleged intermediary, as the sole so-called valid means for seekers to approach God.

Gnostics, on the other hand, fought against the three-tiered system formed inside orthodox

Christianity: theology, ritual, and church hierarchy.

The ancient Gnostics were pragmatic seekers of knowledge and wisdom through human experience. The principles taught by Jesus were more significant to them than the man himself. The historical actuality of Jesus was not of considerable importance. Their main preoccupation, their only guide and ideal, was the mystical and mythical Christ.

To Gnostics, the laws of God, our relationship to Truth and Reality were more significant than the personality of the exponent of those discoveries. To them, the second coming of Christ occurs mystically, within one's own mind. Gnostics like Basilides, Valentinus, Marcus, and Marcion were influential in shaping Gnostic thinking.

Gnosticism, like many other cults and societies, resulted in several schisms due to disagreements in Truth interpretation. Human intelligence cannot comprehend absolute truth. Relative facts have the peculiar property of providing many aspects of Absolute Truth that appear true from one perspective, erroneous from another, and irrelevant from still another.

Certain gnostic manuscripts, including the Gospel of Thomas, were unearthed in Egypt in 1945 at Nag Hammadi. This book is a collection of Jesus' sayings, and some academics regard it as the major source of Jesus' sayings recorded in the four canonical gospels. We will briefly review some of the sayings found in the Gospel.

"Blessed is the lion which a man eats so that the lion becomes a man. But cursed is the man whom a lion eats so that the man becomes a lion." (Gospel of Thomas Saying No.7)

The meaning of this saying is similar to saying No.116:

"Cursed is the flesh that depends on the soul, and cursed is the soul that depends on the flesh!" (Ibid. Saying No.116)

The carnal self, or bestial element within man, is frequently shown as a lion. This symbolism was widely used by alchemical writers in the past. Consuming a lion is a process of transmuting and sublimating man's baser instincts. This is consistent with the evolutionary need suggested by man's spiritual nature's higher impulses.

Allowing animal tendencies to govern and tyrannize the higher qualities of our being, on the other hand, is to metaphorically be swallowed by the lion by allowing its persona to be projected upon our Real Self. In some ways, this is similar to worshiping an idol, a false god who misleads man's senses and consciousness within the maze of Maya.

Man should identify with his Atma, his spiritual nature, rather than believing that his lower principles and their cravings are his Reality. Attachment to the flesh causes anguish and grief, and man is cursed by such conditions that bind his soul to the wheel of life and reincarnation, as Gautama, the Buddha, compassionately pointed out to us.

As a means of escaping the conflict within the spirit, this great messenger of God provided us the eight-fold road. Christ gave us the first commandment to love, which, if lived and applied within our thoughts and feelings, would yoke the fragment to the whole.

"Blessed is the man who has laboured; he has found life!" (Ibid. Saying No.63)

The objective consciousness of man is dying—spiritual death. He moves and thinks like a zombie within God's presence.

Man, blind to spiritual realities and verities, as well as his divine potential, relies excessively on irreligious science and unscientific religion, which dulls as well as stimulates his mind and emotions with an artificial, mechanized way of life that degrades the soul.

Life is Reality, and those seeking the larger life must labor in the vineyard of the soul to awaken consciousness of God's Kingdom. Everything temporal and fleeting is unreal. Nothing in this three-dimensional reality is absolute Reality because everything is in a state of flux, of becoming. The Real remains constant.

The reliance on situations, relationships, and objects in this false world for one's mental and emotional well-being and security eventually breaks the balance of body, mind, and soul, resulting in discord, sickness, and misery. Illness is the absence of Life's abundant force.

God is Life, and Life in man's physical vehicle is found in the blood. Denying God's existence both within and without us is denying the very base of our being, the very life-force of our being.

According to one school of thinking, disintegration occurs on a spiritual level to all of the principles or components that make up man if denial is a persistent state incarnation after incarnation. The closest such an unlucky human might approach to the life-essence, hence God, in order to survive spiritually is through bloodshed. This outlines the heinous acts of individuals who practice blood sacrifices, vampirism, and murder.

Matter presents a significant challenge to the Ego. It provides resistance to its etherealization, control of which honors man with the unfoldment of his Christhood. No other being can do this on our behalf. We brought this circumstance on ourselves by demanding free will in higher planes of existence.

It is man's job and privilege to preserve his soul in order to gain a richer existence, a greater consciousness, a greater state of being, and to secure a permanent place in God's Kingdom as a pillar of perfection.

"He who is near me is near the fire, and he who is far from me is far from the kingdom." (Ibid. Saying No.86)

The fire in this context refers to the spark of God within man's heart. This spark represents the heavenly part of man encased in matter. It is the source of life within the body and correlates to the sun in the solar system. This flame is described by Hindu mystics as a celestial being meditating at the heart of the anahata chakra.

This holy spark is known as "Dahara," which means "minuscule" with "radiant overtones." (Encyclopedic Dictionary of Yoga, by Georg Feuerstein)

The Essenes and Their Influence Upon The Life of Jesus Christ

He who is attuned to the harmony of the Cosmos, Tao, and the Divine I AM feeds and spreads the flame—like the Colombes tending the sacred fire in Vesta's temple—resulting in a greater manifestation of God, the Shekinah, in man's expression in the Malkuth world—Assiah, God's footstool. Man manifests his whole divine potential with the fruits of the Tree of Life in full development with the elements of will/power, love/wisdom, intelligence/activity in equilibrium and total unfoldment, glorified by the divinity of his God-presence.

Heaven, also known as the Kingdom of God, is an inner state, a state of awareness in which peace, harmony, bliss, love, compassion, wisdom, and power reign supreme.

Divine unification with the source of our being causes man's awareness to transcend and carry him into the crown of the larger Flame, the kingdom of Life. This is the unio mystica and ascension sought by Christian mystics and saints since the Master Jesus' resurrection.

The Essenes

There was a pre-Christian sect known as "the Essenes" who were significant in the shaping of Christianity, and we should take a brief look at them.

The Essenes are said to have existed centuries before the arrival of the embodiments of Love and Purity, represented by Jesus and John—the Harbinger.

This distinct branch of the Great White Brotherhood is supposed to have begun in Egypt and is related to the Theraputae, a healing group widespread in the nations surrounding the Mediterranean. Some esoteric historians trace their origins back to Samuel's school of prophets—the Prophet who anointed Saul as King of Israel.

The brethren of this secret group were frequently referred to as "the Mysterious Ones," "the Secret Ones," and "the Silent Ones" due to their mystical rituals, disciplines, behavior, and the expression and habits of their daily secular existence.

An Essene colony previously lived on the banks of Lake Moeris in Egypt. Some of the members were celibates, and those who married most likely engaged in specific spiritual activities that allowed exalted souls to incarnate.

The Essenes, like the Christ initiate, despised animal sacrifice. This mindset was most likely adopted by the former from the latter.

The Essenes had no slaves or servants and lived communally, sharing worldly possessions and cooperating amicably in all endeavors.
They were healers who used herbs, minerals, the "laying of hands," and the invocation of healing angels. Outsiders viewed the members of the community to be saintly and devout.

The Essenes are not referenced in the New Testament save for a few hints about the mysterious men in white who frequently appeared to the disciples of the Nazarene Master to offer advice. The white woolen robes they wore, which imply pre-Islamic Sufism, appear to be a prestige insignia for them as higher degree members.

The Essenes were vegetarians in terms of nutrition; they are also thought to be "God-eaters," a word denoting the ability to nourish the physical body with the life-giving qualities found in the pranic ethers. This, together with their harmonious alignment with other Cosmic forces, may explain their extremely long-life span, which ranges from a hundred to a hundred and twenty years.

Due to the Essenes' secretive and isolated lives, Roman historians such as Pliny alluded to them in their writings in a somewhat hazy manner. The absence of any direct allusions to the Essenes in the Bible is an important aspect to consider.

While other influential sects on Judaic society, such as the Sadducees and Nazarites, were mentioned, the compilers and writers of the gospels for some reason felt it necessary to leave the Essenes out of their texts; or could it be that references to their existence and activities were deliberately omitted from the gospels for political reasons by Church Fathers?

It is worth noting that, while Jesus chastised other sects for their sins, he did not target or condemn the Essenes. Was this done for a valid reason? As a son or initiate of the Mysteries, he had to have known about them.

Some esotericists believe that Jesus' parents, Joseph and Mary, were Essenes. The brotherhood is claimed to have provided Jesus with his early spiritual upbringing. What Jesus taught later in his ministry resembled the Essenes' precepts, doctrines, practices, and disciplines, such as baptism; invocation of higher forces and intelligences; meal blessing; prophecy and healing practice; teachings concerning the Kingdom of God; and angelology, or the science of energy-forces of Nature personified by those beings.

The Essenes emerged unexpectedly on the world stage and then departed, leaving no evidence of their existence. Scholars frequently ask about the reason of the brotherhood's formation. Some speculate, and tradition supports, that the primary goal of the Essene community's establishment was to prepare for the arrival of the Messiah and his work here on Earth.

The Essenes vanished from public view shortly after the Master Jesus vanished. Whether they opted to disband or operate in secret, it is thought that many of their theories found their way to other esoteric schools such as Masonry, the Rosicrucian Brotherhood, the Knights Templar, and many more in following decades.

Extensive scrolls unearthed in a cave at Wadi Qumran along the Dead Sea's coasts in the latter half of this century are likely to give more insight on Essene belief and lifestyle when fully made public.

There is currently a rebirth of the Essenes and what can be considered 'Essenic philosophy' among spiritual occultists.

The Esoteric Life of Jesus

Many aspects of Jesus' hidden esoteric life are unknown to Orthodox Christians. According to them, all significant events in Jesus' life were recorded in the canonical gospels, and further investigation into the matter is undesirable and unnecessary; however, several questions are raised by scholars, the most notable of which are the lack of information on Jesus' spiritual, mystical, and secular training; and the non-chronology of Jesus' activities between the time of his debate with the Doctors of the Law in the Temple at age twelve a.

What happened in the interim? Though exoteric Christianity is deafeningly mute on the matter, the esoteric side, with its psychic research, gives some light. One may readily question the veracity of the information concerning the esoteric side of Jesus' life—we can only say that it is as veracity as the canonical gospels—and there is more to this assertion than a quick awareness can tell.

Much of what follows is based on the book "*The Aquarian Gospel of Jesus*," a manuscript based on what Levi, an American preacher of the nineteenth century, witnessed in the akashic archives.

The events and account of Jesus' life described in the book are supported by the findings of other psychics and scholars. We shall describe the items below and compare them to other data:

Jesus was born to Essene parents and was a typical child in every regard except that he was extraordinarily clever and precocious. Students of esotericism think that the three magi who visited the newborn baby are prior incarnations of spiritual Masters familiar to Theosophists: El Morya, Kuthumi, and Dwal Kul.

The magi saw the Star of Bethlehem, which was esoterically speaking, the highly developed causal body of the Initiate Jesus. However, the Star is more significant.

A poet once wrote of the "trailing clouds of splendor" that follow every child's birth. The cloud that trailed behind the infant destined to be the Christ shone brightly.

In addition, there was a prophecy among the magi that Zarathustra, or Zoroaster, had promised his followers that he would return with his angels to guide them.

It appears that the magi thought Jesus was the reincarnation of Zoroaster.

Throughout Jesus' prenatal and early life, a divine figure appears. He is known as "Gabriel" among the parents of Jesus and John—the Harbinger.

Based on the Essenes' interest in the child Jesus and the characteristic nature of their higher ranked members, Gabriel was most likely one of their holy brethren who was skilled in the practice of bilocation, or psychic projection. This high archangel may have also cast a shadow over one of its comrades.

Whatever form Gabriel took, he was clearly helpful in relaying critical messages and defending the Holy Family from hostile powers.

After learning that an infant had been born and was destined to be "King of Israel," Herod ordered his soldiers to slaughter every child in the kingdom. The parents of Jesus, Joseph and Mary, fled to Egypt, carrying the promised child with them.

So far, the events described are consistent with the canonical gospels; nevertheless, the accounts of Luke, Mark, Matthew, and John neglect to chronicle further developments that were critical to Jesus' spiritual training.

The Masters of the Egyptian Brotherhood taught Mary and her cousin the workings of Cosmic Law and spiritual concepts in Zoan, Egypt.

These diverse teachings were imparted to them with the intention of ultimately passing them on to Jesus and his precursor, John the Harbinger, at the appropriate time. After a few years of educational activities, the mothers were told to return to Israel.

As a child, Jesus enjoyed reading the holy scriptures of the world, such as the Avesta and the Vedas. He was particularly fond of David's Psalms and memorized the majority of what he read.

Following events revealed The Embodiment of Love's nature for the first time in the story.

In honor of Jesus' birthday, his grandparents hosted a feast. When the host inquired about the gift Jesus desired, the youngster appealed on behalf of the starving children in the area. Permission was granted for him to invite the hungry ones to the feast, which filled the young Jesus' heart with gladness.

Even as a child, Jesus condemned the Jewish priesthood's practice of animal sacrifice. When the young Jesus approached Hillel, the chairman of the Sanhedrin, he was unable to console Jesus' broken heart over the blood-ceremony. Hillel, moved by Jesus' earnestness and insight, promised to educate the infant in Jewish exoteric law. Jesus received his early esoteric training from the Essene Brotherhood.

He once grumbled to his mother about the Jews' narrow-mindedness and expressed his wish to meet his "other brothers" in other countries to study their ways. When an Indian Raja visited the region, he invited and offered to support Jesus' mystic-religious study in India.

It would be appropriate at this point to digress for a moment to highlight the many methods by which Jesus' mystical and spiritual training was accomplished. His primary modes of study and knowledge acquisition were as follows:

1) Attunement with the Cosmic Mind, with God's Omniscience.

2) Recollection of knowledge and training from former lifetimes.

3) Personal observation of people, their beliefs, and way of life.

4) Personal research and study of ancient, secret manuscripts.

5) Tutorship under various Masters of Wisdom.

To return to our summary: Jesus taught and studied in India, and it was there that he learned the mystic art of healing. He made friends and enemies among the Arya-Hindus here.

He spoke out against the caste system, infuriating the Brahmins. A friend encouraged him to depart when the situation became too dangerous. Given the circumstances, the young avatar chose to visit Nepal and continue his mission there.

Prior to his departure from India, Jesus learned of his father's death and wrote to his mother to console her. He learned about the presence of secret teachings in Tibet from an Indian Master in Nepal.

He resolved to read the manuscripts for himself and set out for the monastery in Tibet where they were kept. Meng-Tse, a Chinese sage who supported him with his spiritual pursuits, welcomes him cordially in the kingdom of Lamaism.

Certain texts about Jesus' trip in India and Tibet are supposed to have existed at one of the monasteries. The famed Russian painter Nicholas Roerich is reported to have seen or known about these manuscripts.

After a brief sojourn in Tibet, the youthful avatar traveled to his motherland of Nazareth, stopping in Persia and Assyria along the way.

The magi who visited him in Bethlehem when he was a baby welcomed him in Persia. He and several others meditated in quiet on humanity's spiritual needs. Healing and preaching were among his other endeavors in Persia, and afterwards in Assyria.

He taught the "few" Persians a meditational process of mystical development. He toured some ruins in Babylon, Assyria, with Ashbina, a mystic Master of the Land. Soon later, he is on his way home.

Following his reunion with his mother, relatives, and friends, he embarks on another journey, this time to Greece and Egypt.

Like his western forefathers, Plato and Pythagoras, he applied for initiation into the Mysteries of the Egyptian branch of the Great White Brotherhood in Egypt. The Hierophants of the Brotherhood initiate the Nazarene into the deepest secrets of Man, Nature, and God after completing various exams with honors. This culminates in him receiving the title "Christ" upon graduation.

Before departing for Nazareth, the crowned Jesus is blessed by the Seven Sages of that particular world-period and convened to debate the spiritual requirements of man living in the new dispensation of the Piscean Age. The Seven Sages, who formed a "Council of Seven," represented the exoteric rays that emanated from the Great Central Sun. They are related to the "Seven Chohans of the Rays," as they are known in New Age spirituality.

It is believed by mystics that the mission of Jesus consisted of 7 goals:

1) To instruct the masses concerning the immortality of the Soul and salvation from physical bondage by personal effort.

2) To embody and replace the imagery of wrath surrounding God with that of Love.

3) To demonstrate the birth and perfection of the Christ within, followed by the spiritualization of the physical form.

4) To anchor a certain spiritual force into the physical plane and planet.

5) To live out a parable of the Soul.

6) To fulfill the various prophecies concerning the Messiah in the Holy Scriptures.

7) To demonstrate the divine potentiality, the occult talents and powers of Man.

We know from exoteric and esoteric sources that the Nazarene Master successfully completed his spiritual purpose.

Unfortunately, the Church has misunderstood and misinterpreted the Avatar's teachings over the years. The texts, the gospels, were changed for political and personal reasons by the Councils of Nicaea and Trent. Wine that has been poisoned is undrinkable, whether in fresh or old skins.

The nature of gifts is intriguing enough to warrant comment: all blessings come from a spiritual source. God bestows blessings through man. Man can only be a conduit through which God's blessings and grace flow.

Love is the factor that leads man's heart to grant a blessing, and Love, as all mystics know, is an aspect of God's triune essence. Blessings cannot be withdrawn, as shown in the story of Isaac and his sons, Esau and Jacob, because heavenly intellect does not make mistakes. '

Love operates impersonally in accordance with the Law of Karma, the Law of Grace, and the Law of Giving and Forgiving. It is more enjoyable to bless than to curse. The former is an egoistic expression, whereas the latter is a heavenly flow.

Power flows via the hands whether the operator is aware of it or not, hence the hands in their many mudras, or mystic movements, are frequently employed to bestow blessings on others.

The seven Masters blessed the Nazarene by placing their hands, the tools of their will, on Jesus' crown chakra. Invocation to God or the heavenly hierarchy is common in many Esoteric Christian rites, particularly when imparting a divine influence to another.

Divine strength through the hands, divine words given from the cleansed throat chakra, and divine love flowing from the bright anahata chakra all combine to form a powerful force that elevates the awareness of the recipient of the blessing.

It is man's privilege and responsibility to bless every lower life, because the bigger life has gifted man with individuality, self-consciousness, and the potential for immortality; yet, blessings should be given intelligently and discriminately, according to the individual's need.

It is not only the recipient who is blessed by God's grace, but also the giver's grace; the instrument of God's graces is also blessed by the spiritual transmission. Although the blessings we are discussing here are of a psycho-spiritual nature, they may also take on a material shape.

Blessings have creative, productive, and curative benefits, whereas curses are intrinsically destructive—even to the one cursing. Our current culture appears to have lost the desire and inclination to bless. Curses, on the other hand, have become a fake art form, a distorted feeling of pleasure to those undermining the dignity of man's acute sensitivity to Nature's many manifestations.

The Kali-Yuga is a pot of high heat and pressure. All dross eventually and inexorably rises to the surface at the personal and global levels to be dealt with by Man; because Man is the source of the majority of the dark effluvia, the misqualified energies that each Divine

Fragment of God should transmute and cleanse.

Following Jesus' appearance at the Jordan River to be baptized by John—the Harbinger, the narrative follows a pattern similar to the canonical gospels. It is unnecessary to go over this again; instead, we shall look at some of the cryptic teachings of Christian esotericism.

Esoteric Doctrines

Various esoteric schools were founded during the years following the ascension of the Nazarene to maintain the secret teachings of Jesus, by command of the Great White Brotherhood. For fear of being punished by the Church and State, the majority of them functioned in secret.

It was only natural for these Mystery Schools to guard the treasures of the Spirit for the elect, the "selected few," in an Age of superstition, terror, and ignorance. The mystical circles' brethren took a pledge not to cast pearls before swine. Cathars, Rosicrucian, Templars, Alchemists, Christian Kabbalists, Gnostics, and Martinists were among the religious brotherhoods and traditions that taught the underlying meaning and mystical understanding of the Holy Scriptures.

The doctrines and precepts of these distinguished Orders shared teachings, with minor differences in detail and techniques for achieving the spiritual objective, the "Holy Grail": The quest for the Chalice in the Grail stories demanded a warrior's will, discipline, and determination; the purity of a maiden capable of enchanting a unicorn; and the simple faith of a child in tune with Nature—all of these were embodied by Sir Galahad, the only knight successful enough to obtain the Chalice in the Grail Mysteries without difficulty.

At this point, we would want to briefly examine the following esoteric topics:

1) Man's Fall

2) Reincarnation

3) Karma

4) Light

5) Man's Divinity

6) Perfection

7) Salvation

8) The Esoteric Concept of God

The Story of Man's Fall

Man's Fall

In the Western Tradition, there are numerous accounts and interpretations of Man's Fall. This belief is the foundation upon which all other teachings and principles of esotericism are formed; for without a "fall," how could there be a "salvation"? Why should we strive for perfection, wholeness, and unity?

In his current state of existence, man is solitary, alone, and fractured. Man subconsciously experiences a sense of confusion toward Life, Nature, and his fellowmen. He seeks without knowing what he desires. He pursues earthly ambitions, and when they are achieved, he is dissatisfied and unfulfilled. Gradually, he realizes that his energy are being misdirected, that they are being wasted on fleeting pursuits with no absolute value. He then begins his quest and journey toward greater ideals and spiritual endeavors.

But how can one walk the Path of Return? To understand the Way of Ascension, one must first understand how man's descent occurred, how he lost his divine estate. What caused the Fall of Man?

After learning the different traditions passed down by humanity's Bards, each student would arrive at his or her own interpretation and conclusion about what happened at the beginning of time.

Although personal ideas, guesses, assumptions, and convictions are not truths and should not be taken as such, they do provide us with a working knowledge with which to begin our mystical work—especially when inner or spiritual guidance is lacking. We will present the doctrine of Man's Fall based on our level of comprehension:

Universes come and go like any other organism or assemblage. They are formed by Shakti, or God's force, and are sustained for a period of time, a cycle known as "Manvantara," before being dissolved, destroyed, or absorbed back into the Source to be recreated or re-emanated in a "New Day."

It is acceptable to emphasize here that Esoteric Christianity's Cosmo-conception, or cosmology, is primarily emanationist. This suggests that God, or Omniety, created beings and spiritual realms from within ITS own womb.

The emanations, however, do not have autonomous life; everything is an expression or active manifestation of Omniety or "Allah." Omniety is everything, and yet Omniety is so much more. This is God's immanence and transcendence. Separation is an optical illusion, a game of the senses.

Man cannot comprehend the process of Activity and Rest, also known as Manvantara and Pralaya. We will not go into further detail because it would simply add to the confusion.

Humankind, known as "Adam Kadmon" or "Anthropos," was emanated by that tremendous outpouring of Omniety known as "Logos" during one of the active cycles. Adam

Kadmon is the aggregate name of the Fragments that make up its existence.

Scholars have recognized Adam Kadmon as the Creative and Solar Logos. This is debatable, as some mystics have distinguished between the three; possibly it is akin to our physical body, which is made up of cells, each of which is a being, a unit of Life.

Although the physical body is not our Self, it does have its own basic consciousness. The Solar Logos and Adam Kadmon have a similar relationship: the Solar Logos is the Self; the Creative Logos, or collective Elohim—the elemental awareness of the physical body; and the cells are the Fragments, the Monads of Man, or collectively, Adam Kadmon. In past cycles, the fragments of Adam had been personalized and were ready to restart their progress towards Divine Self-Consciousness.

Another Logos to explore is the Redemptory Logos. This being or principle is distinct from the preceding Logoi listed above. This Logos is the "Atma-Buddhi-Higher Mental," jointly known as "the Holy Christ Self," within man, the microcosm.

Prior to Adam Kadmon's emission, the Godhead emitted "Perverse Beings," as Martinez Pasquale termed them. Certain Gnostics refer to them together as "Sacla," "Samael," and "Yaldabaoth." These creatures were the laggards of earlier cycles who did not quite make the cut and were mercifully given another chance to live happily with the Cosmic Laws, which are the laws of their existence and being, and progress accordingly.

A specific esoteric philosophy teaches that disobeying such regulations will eventually cancel their core-identity, the fiery-essence of their identity on "Judgment Day," at the end of the current cycle, if their conversion to holiness (wholeness) is not forthcoming.

This is the "second death," and it is an act of Divine Mercy, because allowing these creatures to continue existing as spirits would bring them unnecessary grief, pain, and suffering—all of which they have caused. Sacla, despite being re-emanated, did not repent, and his evil way of thinking, which had almost become second nature to him, resumed.

He willfully ignored the existence of his source out of pride and ignorance, believing himself to be the creator of the Universe. Sacla's ambition to be worshiped and to behave as the Supreme Being in creating other beings eventually led to his demise. In his book "Esoteric Christian Doctrine," John Bricaud writes regarding the Fall:

" .. *certain heads of the angelic hierarchy refused to obey the laws which govern the pleroma; that they wanted to go over to degrees higher than their class without fulfilling the required condition, which caused great disorder in the pleroma.*"

Anarchy and mayhem resulted from this state of spiritual denial and hostility. As a result, the majority of the angels fell. A entity known variously as "Lucifer," "Athamas," and "Orphiomorphos" led the uprising.

To coerce these fallen angels into compliance would have been a violation of

Omniety's Law of Free Will. To restrain their perversity, their bad intentions, Omniety emitted the lower spiritual planes to circumscribe and contain the actions of these rebels of the spirit; to limit their ability of effect upon the pleroma and higher realms. As a result of egoic-focus, the principles or component elements of these entities were spontaneously densified or crystallized according to natural rules.

In reality, the entirety of Cosmic Laws is the expression of Omniety—is Omniety. Discord with one's spiritual nature naturally densifies the being and limits the mobility of the soul and spirit. This is what happened to Sacla. He degraded and restricted his expression as a result of his rebellion against the rule of his existence.

The nature of evil's low vibrations limits its own extension. This is why no sort of evil can exist in the celestial worlds. The Law of Cause and Effect, not Omniety, was responsible for the punishment. Opposing God's Will is essentially opposing one's own rules of existence. It is wrong to suggest that Omniety punished the fallen angels since this implies that Omniety is directly concerned with, and recognizes, states of duality, which signifies that God is aware of something other than ITS own existence. This is nonsensical from the Absolute point of view, as taught in non-dual philosophies such as Advaita Vedanta. There is only God; everything else is a illusion. This is something that all mystics agree on.

After the rebellion of the angels, Adam Kadmon was re-emanated to continue his journey towards Godhood and to be the warden of the wicked beings, or the director of their progress. Adam was in a state of transition. He was in tune with the Cosmic Mind while also sensing the malevolent ideas of the twisted entities. Although he was born after the perverse beings, he was spiritually "higher" because he was pure—and innocent, because his mental being was still germinal—this was Adam's paradisical bliss—a blissful ignorance, because he had not yet tasted the fruit of the Tree of Knowledge; he had an unawakened mental nature.

Adam, as warden, was intended to instill purity in the wayward entities through his spiritual nature; however, he was affected by their telepathic suggestions of rebellion against the responsibilities at hand. More than that, Sacla convinced Adam that by eating the forbidden fruit, he could become like God and create like Omniety. As a result of his autonomous free will, Adam attempted to create but failed miserably. He made the physical realm of dense stuff known as "Eve." He then filled the plane with shadowy entities unworthy of the Spirit's presence.

The ancient Gnostics held a firm belief that the physical plane was created by someone other than Omniety (God).

The "Demiurge," an imperfect creator, produced an imperfect hylic world. However, this circumstance provided the Fragments with a greater possibility for rapid growth. Exoterically, "The Great Architect of the Universe," the Demiurge, or P'an Ku, as Chinese thinkers refer to him, was a contributing cause of the bondage of his constituent parts, in the same way that our inharmonious thoughts and sentiments can make the cells of our body a slave to poor health. T.G.A.O.T.U, on the other hand, is a Cosmic evolution mastermind. Matter, despite its resistance to control by interacting intelligences, provides spiritual discipline to youthful souls.

Adam was charmed by his creation to the point where it progressively captured him. The metaphor of Narcissus, who was so enthralled and fascinated by his own reflection in a pond that he plunged into it and died spiritually, exemplifies this state in the Greek Mysteries.

Adam had forgotten his true identity while identifying with his caricature. All of his former abilities had vanished in the veil of Self-forgetfulness. The misuse of free will caused his Fall, and his ignorance, his self-forgetfulness, comprised the "original sin."

His "punishment" was harsher than that of the rebel angels of the angelic hierarchy because he carried out his nefarious plans to fruition, which the rebel angels did not have the opportunity to do.

The Fall of Man is dramatized in numerous ancient Mystery Schools, including the myth of the slain hero-god and Persephone's capture and rape. The story of the crucified Christ is simply a reenactment of a Cosmic event that occurred before time.

Before his fall, Adam was unaware of his Source. Because he was unenlightened, he thought of himself as the supreme being, much like Sacla before him. The main causes of his captivity within the tomb of matter were pride, want, and ignorance. This condition of mind, this degree of consciousness, may be found in today's masses.

Many people are unaware of man's divine potential, the Cosmic verities, the existence of an Absolute Supreme Being, higher intelligences, and the spiritual worlds; and this unfortunate state causes their energy-forces to be misdirected into thoughts and actions that are detrimental to their spiritual well-being.

From one perspective, Man has never truly left his Edenic state. The apple he ate caused him to believe he was separated from his Source. His consciousness is obscured by what we call "Maya-grams," or "forms of unreality" by our definition—and these Mayagrams are perfectly real to man.

The Mayagrams are fleeting, the substance of which dreams are fashioned; Absolute Reality is eternal.

Man pushes his Edenic-Reality to the back of his mind and hypnotizes himself with transient things; as a result, he appears to be devoid of heavenly attributes and faculties.

From one point of view, the serpent that lured Man to eat the apple—the fruit of forgetfulness—as related in the allegorical book of Genesis reflects the Law of Evolution, the creative drive of the pulsing Center of All. In the Mystery Schools, this is depicted by a serpent coiling an egg. The evolutionary force inherent within Life, inside Man's nature, that prompted him to descend into matter, unfold his divinity, and ascend to his God-estate, is the basis of this sign.

The perverse entities eventually joined man on the physical realm, and they are still with us now. Their typical evil, with which we are all familiar, has a great influence in the political, economic, social, scientific, and religious areas. As a result, humankind is roughly and symbolically divided into two lineages: the perverse humans, the "descendants of Cain," and the Fragments of Adam Kadmon, the "posterity of Seth." According to Esoteric Christianity, there are three classifications of man:

1) Hylic, the individual who lives solely according to his carnal nature, "the dead," as designated by Jesus.

2) Pneumatic, the individual who lives in accord with his spiritual being, the type of personality called by Jesus, "the quick."

3) Psychic, the individual who lives in an intermediary state, or what Jesus called "lukewarm."

The three basic human natures are listed above. Man, on the other hand, does not only represent the human race. Angels, fallen angels, titans, and other entities have been incarnated as Adam Kadmon. As described in Genesis and the Books of Enoch, the "sons of God" did cohabit with human spirits to generate hybrids.

In the Qabalah, the entire drama of Man's Fall correlates to the four worlds or stages of development:

1) Atziluth, the World of Archetypes, corresponds with the impetus and commencement of a new Manvantara.

2) Briah, the World of Creation, corresponds with the emanations of beings, the period of the rebellion of the angels.

3) Yetzirah, the World of Formation, corresponds with the creation of the lower spiritual realms and the actual fall of the rebel angels.

4) Assiah, the World of Activity, corresponds with the creation of the physical plane and the Fall of Man.

The Doctrines of Reincarnation and Karma

Reincarnation

In this universe, everything is in motion. Movement causes transformation or change. This is an unchanging everlasting constant, a Law of the Cosmos. The transformation process occurs in stages, phases, and cycles.

According to the Law of Activity and Rest, every unit of life develops its consciousness. The cycle of activity begins with birth, youth, and maturity, and concludes with so-called death, which is the era of Rest. The cycle is repeated until the goal for that life-unit is met. Reincarnation is a manifestation of the Law of Activity and Rest in human evolution. It is known as "Gilgul" in Jewish mysticism and was taught by the Greek philosophers Plato, Pythagoras, and Plotinus. Most of the world's religious writings contain references to the law, albeit some are hidden.

When man got entombed within Matter, it became necessary for him to free himself. However, according to our observations, mankind as a whole is not pursuing this aim since he is unaware of the purpose of his existence. The Inner Self's promptings are misconstrued as the selfish ambitions of the personal ego. In some ways, having a physical body is a great advantage since it allows for quick spiritual development. But it would be foolish to prolong our stay in the world of matter. This plane of consciousness is only a stage on the path to our spiritual destiny. Larger effort, greater tasks await us somewhere in the cosmos' vast reaches. We must acknowledge that the physical world is not our true home. We are spiritual creatures who have spiritual ancestors.

Ignorance and egoistic desire are the two negative forces that keep us bound to the wheel of birth and reincarnation. As our personal will and consciousness become connected with the Divine Will and Mind of our True SELF, we gain spiritual freedom.

Causes bind us to the wheel of rebirth. Every situation has two sides. We've already discussed the negative factors. Positive causes include our desire for excellence and the balancing of karma. The Soul's intentional will is the first positive cause, as human perfection can be advanced by interacting with and masterfully overcoming matter's opposition.

Karma binds us to the wheel until its erroneous energy is expended, balanced, and compensated, or the Law of Grace is invoked to override the karmic condition as a result of spiritually learning the required lesson that the Law anticipated one to learn.

The concept of a human soul being born cyclically into the physical world is known as reincarnation. But there are numerous titles for reincarnation, each with a slightly different meaning and implication. These are the following terms: rebirth, reimbodiment, transmigration, and metempsychosis. The term transmigration frequently conjures up images of retrogression, of man re-embodying as an animal. This is a spiritual impossibility since the human spirit, once personalized, can never revert to an undivided animal soul. The animal vehicle cannot bear the enormous radiation and magnets of the human personalized Spirit.

This concept of retrogression, or the transmigration of the human soul into an animal form, is a misunderstanding of a doctrine that teaches the similarity of human characteristics to animal nature, which is retained embodiment after embodiment until the energies underlying the bestial nature are transmuted.

Thoughts and feelings can also greatly influence and shape the astral form. They tend to reflect the soul's essence. If the human spirit is beastly in nature, the astral body will reflect that. When the lower components of the soul, the astral and etheric bodies, are discarded by the human spirit, they may gravitate to similar environments and objects. Thus, we may have the prospect of these ethereal cadavers attaching themselves to animals—this is likely where the concept of humans incarnating as animals originated.

If reincarnation is a Cosmic rule, a doctrine of Truth, why is it not taught by the priesthood in churches? This is a prevalent question among exoteric church members.

Unbeknownst to them, this teaching was a fundamental principle of the early Church, and allusions to it abound in the scriptures and gospels. St. Augustine, St. Clement, and Origen all believed and understood the theory of reincarnation. So did Ptolemaic Bishop of Synesius (370-430 AD). St. Gregory of Nyssa (257-333 AD) was a firm believer in the rule of law, writing:

"It is absolutely necessary that the soul be healed and purified, and if this does not take place during its life on earth it must be accomplished in future lives."

In his literary writings, Origen expounded on the law. He wrote a lot about the Law of Re-embodiment. However, in following decades, the mystical doctrines of Origen were anathemized in the Council of Constantinople in 553 AD, and numerous references to reincarnation in the gospels were removed.

This Council, presided over by Emperor Justinian and boycotted by the reigning Pope, was a parody of the Council of Sages, which meets on a regular basis under the auspices of the Great White Brotherhood.

The participating bishops of this Council agreed to the dogmas drafted by Justinian and his co-conspirators, with the majority of them doing so out of fear of the Emperor.

The Doctrine of Reincarnation was rejected because it contradicted the dogmas that the Emperor and his bishopric circle desired to promote: eternal damnation, vicarious atonement, resurrection, and Jesus' uniqueness as God's "single" son.

The conspirators denounced reincarnation at this Council in order to gain greater political power and corrupt men's minds.

The assenting bishops were not cross-bearers for the Master Jesus. Their terror outweighed their affection for him. Their lack of bravery and action initiated and perpetuated a deception that continues to mislead the flock of Christ to this day.

This deception fosters a spiritual slothfulness and fearful attitude in which redemption is looked for and dependent on others rather than one's own mystical resources.

One of the issues that the Gnostics and the exoteric Church disagreed on was reincarnation. Before being translated and altered by people affected by newly formed creeds and dogmas, the original holy scriptures and gospels contained positive allusions to the Law of Reincarnation as taught by the Nazarene Master. However, certain reincarnation-related material remains in the translated, distorted books.

Due to intolerance, racism, and the limitations that they impose on their consciousness, some biblical students are unable or unwilling to see the implied law in these texts. This results in a lack of spiritual discernment and comprehension, which are required to intuitively read between the lines and extract the essential meaning. These intriguing passages will be quoted later.

It is critical to remember that not all of Jesus' teachings were recorded in the canonical gospels. The majority of his secret teachings were passed down orally, and some of his oral teachings have found their way into current mystical institutions and fraternities.

We should also not ignore the presence of hundreds of additional passages that were arbitrarily dubbed "apocryphal" or even "works of the devil" and were not included in the Bible because they contradicted the dogmas that the priesthood wanted to propagate. Some of these texts include gleaming diamonds of Gupta Vidya, or Ancient Wisdom.

How is the veracity of reincarnation established? Based on personal experience. This necessitates mystical development with a certain degree of progression down the path of evolution, the Path of Initiation. Some people who believe in reincarnation are overly concerned with discovering their true identity. This is illogical because their current identity has yet to be discovered, realized, and known.

Why waste time and effort on something that would happen organically over time when more vital concerns, such as Self-Realization, await one's attention? It is risky to enter the mind prematurely in order to recall former incarnations using instruments such as hypnotic regression, medications, and others of a similar sort.

Nature has certainly created the human psychosomatic system and circuitry in such a way that man would forget his previous lives for an important reason: to maintain mental poise and balance.

Man drinks the Waters of Lethe at each embodiment to forget harsh events from the soul's past. Prematurely awakening these memories would simply disrupt the individual's psychological stability and sanity, while also enhancing egoistic emotions of vanity, pride, and a false sense of superiority.

Nature does not and will not withhold knowledge and information from man when he reaches a particular stage of development and maturity. Man will recollect former lives without the use of force or artificial interference with his psyche, without becoming a psychiatric patient.

Those who provide psychic readings and hypnotic regression sessions to individuals should be aware of the potentially grave implications of their acts, since these would flood their patients' psyches with buried data that their consciousness may not yet be ready or able to manage.

However, without firsthand experiences, man would always have concerns about the Law of Reincarnation, especially if he has not accepted life beyond so-called death. From that perspective, reincarnation appears to be a fantasy. Fortunately, there are ways to strengthen one's confidence and faith in the law, no matter how flimsy those views may be.

The truth is not only found outside, but also within. The truth seeker will conduct a rational investigation using less dangerous means than hypnosis to determine the accuracy of spiritual principles revealed to man by higher intelligences.

The student's primary research and method of inquiry would most likely be along the lines of reason, objectivity, a study of scriptural revelation; a study of those who have spiritual experiences and understanding—those with spiritual authority; and a study of the phenomenon of spontaneous recollections.

Along the lines of logic, we can begin our investigation by looking into the numerous inequities, complexity, and differences among the sons of man: Why are some people born rich while others are born poor? Why are some people born healthy in mind and body while others are born with physical or mental handicaps? How do we account for the phenomena of child prodigies? How can we address the issue of varying mental capacities, as well as the diverse moral, cultural, and spiritual standards that each individual demonstrates? Education, environment, and genes are small components that do not entirely explain life as we know it. Why does it appear that God has favorites? For example, Jacob triumphed against Esau.

The law of reincarnation fills a void, the missing link that connects the many aspects of our understanding of individual inequality. The expression of the laws of karma and reincarnation is the many sorts of man and their point of progress. One appears to come into this world to spend a brief existence and then leave without accomplishing one's ambitions. What is the point of this? If one's aspirations are impossible in a single lifetime, then our existence here is useless and pointless.

Continuing our logic, we would see God's kindness and grace at work in our lives, and that reincarnation is the manifestation of that mercy and love.

As previously stated, the gospels and Jewish scriptures are rife with references to the law of reincarnation. Here are a few examples, verses frequently cited by law students and researchers:

"I will make him a pillar in the temple of my God; and he shall go no more out." (Rev 3:12)

This verse implies and represents that the individual who frees himself from the bonds of matter engages in active labor in the spiritual realms, guiding the energies and powers of Nature in accordance with the Grand Design, God's Plan and Will.

The attainment of liberation or salvation ensures personal emancipation from the cycle of birth and reincarnation, also known as samsara. A liberated creature is no longer compelled to reincarnate; instead, he goes "no further out," unless it is to help less advanced individuals.

"Behold I will send you Elijah the prophet before the coming of the great and dreadful day of the Lord." (Malachi 4:5)

Elijah's appearance occurred through reincarnation in the form of John the Baptist. Jesus had this to say concerning John's true identity:

". . . Truly, I say to you, among those born of women there has risen no one greater than John the Baptist . . . all the prophets and the law prophesied unto John, and if you are willing to accept it, he is Elijah who was to come . . . " (Matt 11:7-15)

Some biblical scholars believe that Elijah's rebirth was an exception rather than a natural law; yet the overall principle or law was not rejected by the Nazarene Master. In certain gospel texts, he freely discusses it with his disciples:

"'whom do man say that the Son of Man is?' And they said, 'some say John the Baptist, others say Elijah, and others Jeremiah or one of the prophets.' He said to them, 'But whom do you say I am?' Simon Peter replied: 'You are the Christ, the son of the Living God.' And Jesus answered to him, 'Blessed are you, Simon Bar-Jona! For Flesh and blood has not revealed this to you, but my father who is in heaven. And I tell you, you are Peter. And on this rock I will build my church; and the powers of death shall not prevail against it . . . '" (Matt 16:13--20)

Though Jesus taught reincarnation, we believe he intended to emphasize the potential of man obtaining Christhood in a single lifetime and therefore attaining redemption without the need for reincarnation. In the preceding stanza, Jesus discloses to Simon his former identity as Peter.

The expression "on this rock" has a twofold meaning. "Peter" means "rock," but the rock that "death shall not overcome" is the law of reincarnation that Jesus was referring to, and this was supposed to become one of his Church's foundations, its foundation.

Another Exodus verse demonstrates the connection between rebirth and karma:

" . . . Keeping mercy for thousands, forgiving iniquity and transgression, and sin, and that will by no means clear the guilty;

53

visiting the iniquity of the fathers upon the
children, and upon the children's children,
unto the third and to the fourth generation."
(Exodus 34:7)

If taken literally, this text portrays Jehovah as lacking in genuine mercy; after all, why should an innocent offspring suffer for the misdeeds of its progenitor?

The above verse's karmic retribution meted out to the children and children's children refers to the karmic payback that the reincarnating "Ego" must pay in subsequent embodiments.

Karma

Karma is the Law of Cause and Effect, often known as the "law of consequence" or the "law of equilibrium." It is the law of "as ye sow, so shall ye reap" that Jesus and Paul instilled in the masses. According to Jesus:

"With what measure you mete it shall be measured to you again." (Matt 7:2)

Jesus is actually implying that we should be responsible for the burden of our sins.

We are also told in Galatians that,

" . . . every man shall bear his own burden."
(Gal 6:5)

Every man must confront the repercussions of his own actions, whether in thought, speech, or deed. The Master's own statements contradict the belief that one only has to have faith or believe in Jesus to be saved from sin. The authentic teachings of Jesus exhort us to spiritual maturity and independence from others.

It is mentioned in the Book of Jubilees, an apocryphal text, how the higher law deals with man:

"With the instrument with which a man killeth his neighbour with the same shall he be killed; after the manner that he wounded him, in like manner shall they deal with him."

Karma is a manifestation of divine justice and mercy. Aside from being a contributing influence on a person's evolution, it is one of the omniverse's constants that applies and is readily visible acting in the domain of physics.

The law, contrary to popular belief, is impersonal, unbiased, and does not punish; rather, it teaches and educates. It makes a person see the folly of his actions as well as the goodness of his good works. It demonstrates to a person the relationship between acts and their effects. Negative activities have negative consequences, while positive actions have positive consequences.

Karma is God's weapon for balancing out perturbations in the Tao's harmony. The Law declares, in what appears to be harsh terms:

"Vengeance is mine, I will repay . . ." *(Romans 12:19)*

Each person generates karma by his or her everyday thoughts, statements, and acts. No being lives without creating karma, because no being lives without setting forces in motion in his or her daily life.

Simply breathing is karmic in one sense, because every breath has an effect, an outcome in the physical body. Karma is a person's self-made destiny

A Christian of esotericism believes in the presence of the law because he sees its manifestations in his daily life. To such a person, the orthodox Christian belief of "remission of sins" is incompatible with the rule of Karma and is viewed as a notion developed by the Church to control the minds of the public. The only way to avoid unpleasant outcomes is to avoid initiating harmful causes. "Ahimsa," or harmlessness, should be the devout's continual expression—"to turn the other cheek."

Unless one is detached to one's acts, karma binds one to the wheel of birth and rebirth; "vairagya" or detachment is a required virtue commonly taught by Gurus to their chelas to acquire. The entire philosophy and practice of Karma Yoga, as taught by the avatar Sri Krishna in the Bhagavad Gita, is being detached from one's acts. Eastern beliefs may be the greatest way to understand karma.

Karma is classified into three categories. According to Hindu philosophy, they are classified as follows:

- Sattvika Karma, where the results of one's actions are not desired, where one is unattached to them.

- Rajasa Karma, where acts are performed sensuously for the desire of their fruits and rewards.

- Tamasa Karma, where forces are put into motion out of ignorance, confusion, and delusion, without any real care and concern for the consequences of one's deeds.

The Violet Flame of the Holy Spirit

The knowledge of Karma as revealed to the masses by Jesus is a refinement on the previous dispensation's interpretation and understanding of "an eye for an eye, a tooth for a tooth," as taught to the Israelites by Moses.

To illustrate, the law does not impose blindness as a punishment on someone who has previously blinded someone. It does, however, make him aware of the wrongness of his actions—even if blinding him is required if other methods fail to make him understand his error.

If the individual realizes his error, honestly repents, and compensates, the lesson has been learned; he has set in action new forces that counteract the original negative urge.

Karma is not a punitive force. Positive causes mitigate negative karma to some extent; these are the rules of grace and mercy at work. In contrast, even if karma balancing occurs and the individual does not learn, repent, and compensate for his wrongdoings, he may repeat it or the "punishment" may simply occur again and again, lifetime after lifetime, depending on the proportion and momentum of the original force, until all of its misqualified energy is spent.

In addition, undigested and unassimilated experiences are repeated until the essential lesson that the experience is meant to convey is absorbed.

Every entity or collection of beings generates karma, which is why we have terms like "group karma," "race karma," and "national karma."

Karma operates according to cyclic law and esoteric astrological alignments. Its consequences are determined by the ratio of forces set in motion and the situation in which the crimes were committed. Some impacts are immediate, while others take time for the force to return full circle, sometimes even deferring until a subsequent lifetime.

Karma is so conditioned in its entirety and is separated into two categories:

1) Ripe Karma, where the effects of deeds and actions occur in the same lifetime.

2) Unripe Karma, where effects of deeds and actions are postponed to a future embodiment.

According to one modern school of Esoteric Christianity, the Cosmic Directors of Karma granted a dispensation in our century for the spiritual aspirant to transmute his karmic crimes and proclivities.

This dispensation takes the form of an invocation (which Hindus and Buddhists have been utilizing for ages) to the aspect of the Holy Spirit known as the "violet flame." This is God's "devouring fire," as described in the Bible.

When activated in one's energy field, the violet flame transmutes the source, effect, record, and memory of sin and karma until one becomes immaculate:

"Come now, and let us reason together, saith the LORD: though your sins be as scarlet, they shall be as white as snow; though they be red like crimson, they shall be as wool." (Isa: 1:18)

The violet fire's effects lead us one step closer to perfection and ascension into God-Presence. When a disciple is free of personal karma, he or she is ready to take on a greater responsibility of transmuting world karma to some extent, in order to help suffering humanity progress towards the light. This is exactly what the Master Jesus did. He transmuted some of the globe's karma, esoterically "saving the world."

Much work needs to be done, and the individual remains responsible for his crimes and karma—the quality, nature, and status of his own energy-field, his soul-record—which was not cleansed by the "savior's" death. The Master Jesus "killed" for the sake of awakening Man's collective consciousness, not for the salvation of any individual.

Overcoming karma in one's life necessitates a comprehension of the conditions one finds himself in, as well as a constant vigil and check of any inharmonious manifestations of our being. Moderation in all sensual pursuits substantially aids in the reduction of negative fruit such as pain and suffering.

Following are some tips for minimizing karmic influences:

1) Invoke the violet flame on a regular basis.

2) Control of the mind and emotions.

3) Act, think, and speak beneficially.

4) Offer oneself to selfless service to humankind.

5) Be unattached to the fruits of actions.

6) Steer the mind away from sensuality by focusing on one's divinity.

7) Seek spiritual wisdom and teaching in one's life-experiences.

Light

Light manifests in man's mind as illumination, enlightenment, and consciousness expansion. Light, as Truth, is the enlightening mystery bestowed upon Christian Mysteries aspirants who have previously completed the needed perfection, the era of spiritual cleaning.

Those who were free of the taint of sin were offered the Light's secrets for further advancement along the path of ascension, because sinlessness alone was insufficient to lift man to the doors of God's Kingdom and thereby link him with his "I AM Presence."

Jesus says regarding the illuminating secrets in the gnostic classic Pistis Sophia:

"But amen, amen, I say unto you: even if a righteous man hath committed no sin at all, he cannot possibly be brought into the light-kingdom, because the sign of the kingdom of

the mysteries is not with him. In a word, it is impossible to bring souls into the light without the mysteries of the light kingdom."

The Christ initiate also explains one of the key reasons of the Mysteries of Light that man should seek rather than the baubles of this transient world in the same gnostic work:

"For this cause have I said unto you aforetime: 'Seek, that you may find.' I have therefore said unto you: 'You are to seek after the mysteries of this light which purifies the body of matter and make it into a refined light exceedingly purified.'"

"For this corruptible must put on incorruption, and this mortal must put on immortality." (1Cor 15:53)

The foregoing verses are about the etherealization of man's physical component. It is common practice among Esoteric Christians to surround themselves with light during visualizations and meditations for alchemical and spiritual conversion. The precipitation of light particles within one's being not only heals and purifies the aura, but it also accelerates the vibratory rate of our numerous sheaths, or bodies of the Soul and Spirit. The spiritual aspirant should continuously invoke the light that purifies and illuminates. Purifying and spiritualizing the atomic particles that make up one's existence with divine fire is only one of the spiritual transformative processes; the other part is the effort of not assimilating extra coarse stuff. Jesus instructs us to:

" . . . renounce the whole world and all of its association, that ye may   not amass

additional matter to the rest of your matter in
you . . . "

This surrender does not include giving or
selling one's earthly possessions and living in
poverty as an anchorite or a wanderer. The rich
man whom Jesus encouraged to sell his
possessions and join him had a different
meaning. "To be in this world but not of it"
clarifies the preceding precept, implying
detachment, earthly desirelessness,
harmlessness, soul-purpose living, and so
forth. It makes no difference whether one is
rich or poor, well-known or unknown. It is how
we live our lives that matters.

The Pistis Sophia, like Patanjali's aphorisms,
encourages us to avoid many vices such as
slander, conceit and haughtiness, love of the
world, cursing fury, pitilessness, avarice, and
laziness. To renounce vices and develop
virtues, one should reflect on the sanctity and
sacredness of God, Nature, Life, and the
intrinsic nature of all sentient beings. His focus
should be shifted from a worldly three-
dimensional vision and habitual pattern to a
spiritual outlook and style of living. By always
living from a spiritual position, man attains
that level of harmony, that liberation from the
disordered mentality and emotionalism that
defines the worldly man.

Harmony is organization—organized
thought, speech, action, living, and movement.
The light of the godhead's trinity knocks on the
door of waking consciousness and waits.

Harmony within the four lower bodies,
which mirrors Tao harmony, in conjunction
with certain spiritual activities opens the

etheric valves, allowing greater influx of spiritual forces, magnetizing the lower sheaths of man's energy-structure with an abundance of power, love, and knowledge.

Divine powers enter man's being through the Sutratman, antahkarana, and sahasrara chakras.

Man becomes a living flame after being illuminated by the Light of God. He exists as a center of Omniety's heavenly presence. His Divine Self's radiance, attraction, and power fill his aura to the point where his *"cup runneth over,"* and his very presence impacts everybody with whom he comes into contact. God's nature and desire is to turn men into *"flames of fire"* (Heb 1:7).

Each enlightened person, like a Flame of Fire, awakens other souls dormant in the mayagrammic world. This stimulation occurs on all levels of being through magnetic and telepathic induction. We may allow the "dead" to bury the dead, but it is our personal responsibility as torchbearers to resuscitate those who require awakening and resurrection.

Light is the essence of all stuff, according to cosmology. It is the primal energy that manifests in the substances that make up our universe. Matter is densified light. God-radiance manifests in various intensities between materiality and the pure Light of Omniety.

Light was the first emanation of Omniety; it is the manifestation of the Supreme Godhead's first stated creative urge, "Let there be Light." (Gen 1:3). This decree was not the result of the sun and its radiating powers, but of something deeper and loftier.

Light is frequently associated with the Pranava "OM," which reverberates indefinitely throughout the cosmos. The Sound is referred to as "Sabda Brahma" by Hindu mystics.

The Sufis are aware of the presence of this Word-Light; they call it the "Kalam-I-Aadim," which translates as "the Ancient Sound." Christian mystics, on the other hand, refer to it as "the Rush of a Mighty Wind" and "the Sound of the Trumpet."

Gnostics, Hindu and Buddhist Tantric mystics, and High-degree Sufis initiate aspirants into the gnosis or marifat, where the Divine Light and Sound flowing from one's very core being, the very essence of God, are experientially seen and heard.

Blind faith and beliefs are replaced with knowledge, experience, and conviction. One sees God's dazzling aspect face to face and is transformed; the onlooker is no longer a mortal or lives as one but is spiritually immortal as he "sees" his very SELF as "Sat-Chit-Ananda," or "Existence-Consciousness-Bliss."

"Blessed are the pure in heart: for they shall see God. (Matt 5:8)

"And though after my skin worms destroy this body, yet in my flesh shall I see God" (Job 19:26)

"And he said, Thou canst not see my face: for there shall no man see me, and live." (Ex: 33:20)

"And the LORD spake unto Moses face to face, as a man speaketh unto his friend." (Ex 33:11)

Indeed, once one has realized one's basic SELF, one's "I AM PRESENCE," one is never the same again; one no longer lives as a man or as a mere mortal. One becomes the anointed, a Christ, an immortal god, Job's and the Pure's hope. Isn't this what was asked of us:

" . . . I am the way, the truth, and the life: no man cometh unto the Father, but by me." (John 14:6)

Or in other words,

"I AM the true model and I represent the true way of attaining that Divine State of Sonship. Become as 'I AM.'"

This possibility is the essence of the gospel; it is the good news, the kingdom come, the Resurrection, and the Second Coming. This is the promised Kingdom of God, not an astral realm to be entered into in the afterlife or during the Apocalypse in the end times. The kingdom of God is NOW to be gained by everyone, regardless of religious allegiance. May we all take this to heart and live lives with meaning.

Man's Divinity

The Christ Initiate informed the inner circle of his followers about man's true essence and reality in hushed tones. Some of his statements about man can be found in the gospels.

His enigmatic words regarding his relationship with his father were statements of truth that applied to humanity as a whole and were never intended to imply to the public that he was a unique "son of God." As a result of this misinterpretation, perhaps on purpose, of the Master's words, modern Christians worship the son in the form of Jesus rather than in the light of Christ divinity within.

The precepts of man's divinity have been disregarded, misconstrued, and misrepresented throughout the centuries. The human, mortal, sinful side has been overemphasized to a sickening degree.

The Light gleamed in the darkness, but the darkness was unconcerned about its origin or source. There are individuals who fear Light in the form of truth because its nature discloses the genuine state of things—things that are unsettling to those who despise upward spirals achieved via personal effort.

Men were declared to be gods by Jesus and other prophets before him:

"I have said, Ye are gods; and all of you are children of the most High." (Psalms 82:6)

"Shew the things that are to come hereafter, that we may know that ye are gods: yea, do good, or do evil, that we may be dismayed, and behold it together." (Isa 41:23)

"Jesus answered them, Is it not written in your law, I said, Ye are gods?" (John:10:34)

The "Thou art That" declaration of various Hindu ideologies echoes the idea that we are more than mortals. This divine commandment of man's divinity is rejected by orthodox Christians as a doctrine of the devil and is not acknowledged to be true due to their erroneous interpretation of the scriptures and their reliance on dogmas and creeds unilaterally formed by corrupted theologians.

People are brainwashed into believing in things that do not reflect reality, and which cannot be validated by firsthand experience. Where there is a lack of intuitive insight, where ignorance and fanaticism reign, the mind and emotions will cause the jiva or soul to become stuck in a quagmire of their own making. This imposes self-limitation and self-restriction, as well as the self-restriction represented in Plato's Cave allegory.

Man believes what he wants to believe, and he will continue to face the torments of "hell"—pain, misery, dread, and anguish—until he replaces his beliefs and fancies with experiential awareness of his divinity. Herein lies evil, for evil opposes all acts that liberate the soul from its relationship with matter, preventing it from progressing on the path of evolution; therefore man swims subconsciously against the currents that would bring him to the other shore.

Atheistic scientists regard man as a matter being; religionists regard man as a creation, a creature fabricated by the Source for the purpose of glorifying and worshipping Itself by making Its creatures sing hymns of praise forever, for the benefit of who knows whom—for that which is egoless requires no recognition of its SELF-existence, as It is in a state of completeness, of oneness with the hidden nature of its illusory elements as perceived by man. Prayers and worship are never for the advantage of God, but for the beings that are engaged in honored adoration.

We learn about the world's sages from their firsthand experiences of what man truly is, and by following in their footsteps, we get to know ourselves. The sages give strategies for knowing the gnosis, or the Truth. By employing their methodologies, we progressively acknowledge the veracity of their comments about man, some of which were made while in transcendental states. The reasoning for Jesus' previous remark, "I Am the Way, the Truth, and the Life," can be readily comprehended by the intuitive sense.

Most individuals, at the cost of their spiritual development, focus their consciousness, their attention, disproportionately on externals, on a world of illusions. This preoccupation with earthly trinkets depletes the mind, body, and soul of the energies required to bring forth the treasures stored in heaven by man's devotion to the laws of the Voice of Silence.

Christ is the cosmic nature that exists within each individual; the so-called second coming of Christ takes place within the psyche, where man perceives and manifests his own reality in the world of form, in the Malkuth sphere. Constantly focusing inward, as in meditation and certain forms of yoga, allows one to keep the necessary amount of force to awaken and stir the Shekinah, the flickering fire of God's manifestation within man, which resides in his heart chakra as the tripartite flame of Love, Wisdom, and Power.

As a spark, man arose from the fiery center of the Great Central Sun, or "Parabrahm" in Hindu Philosophy. This spark, this "unit" of Brahman, is divine in its essence. It is a representation of God-in-the-making. The Divine Ego, or Atma, was generated and personalized as Self-consciousness from this monadic spark. It has three personalities: the heavenly spirit, the living spirit, and the human spirit.

The Christ in man is the higher part of the Divine Ego, the path to oneness with the Father in heaven, the Monad centered in celestial planes. In Hinduism's Samkhya theory, this Monad is Ishvara.

The Divine Ego creates the personality, the jiva, which manifests as man in the lower worlds of matter. A component of Egoic consciousness is buried in the etheric heart, waiting for the outer consciousness to recognize it and exhibit its essential qualities and nature in the physical plane. Its development is based on the personality allowing it to express itself freely in its field of action.

"Man is God, and God is Man."

This is a metaphysical truism that should be grasped mystically. If taken literally, this spiritual truth appears heretical. God is everlasting and limitless, as is man, because man represents the spiritual structure of the broader cosmos.

Enlightened people recognize God as unfathomable and indescribable. When contemplating man's ultimate essence, one finds oneself in a similar position: Man transcends language; it is impossible to express what is beyond and void of physical, emotional, and mental structures.

Egoism manifests itself in the depreciation of the actual ego and the exaltation of the false ego. Indulging in such states of mind precludes spiritual awakening. Man incorrectly identifies himself with the components of his material manifestations. For example, he believes he is the body, the sensations, the mind, and so on.

This misidentification halts the development of his divinity's abilities and powers, which develop inside man at the objective consciousness level as he gains a better understanding of his real existence and expands his consciousness to cover higher states.

Egoism is an idol that man unconsciously worships on the altar of his consciousness; and each time he thinks, talks, and acts inadequately, adversely, uncultured, and destructively, he exalts the deceiver of men, the beast whose number is 666.

Developing Divinity

Perfection

"Be ye therefore perfect, even as your Father which is in heaven is perfect." (Matt 5:48)

The Nazarene Master spoke the following verse to the masses, who had ignored the relevance and importance of the mandate for generations. Even the priesthood does not appear to emphasize this commandment, instead teaching the incorrect premise of man's original wicked nature and redemption by an external savior.

We were allegedly born in sin, live in sin, and die in sin, and there is no possibility for us to be redeemed from eternal damnation in hell unless we establish a blind confidence in the divinity and single sonship of God of a specific individual.

This view contradicts a number of Jesus' esoteric teachings, including the declaration in Genesis that God created man—gods, according to Psalms—and recognized that his creation was good. Why do we perceive something as awful when God perceives it as good? We certainly see imperfectly since we only see the form and not the essence.

To the progressive mind, the quotation above alludes to the law of evolution and one's efforts to accelerate one's spiritual development. Within the form of each life-unit, perfection is the destiny and purpose of life. In the first stanza of this chapter, "Father" signifies the paradigm of man, Adam Kadmon, the spiritual image into which each human awareness is to grow.

Man was created as a spark of God, with a perfect blueprint as his spiritual identity. Man is to reflect the identity and traits of the macrocosm within his lower self in order to exhibit that perfection in the realm of form. Because it is impossible to achieve perfection in a single embodiment, Nature has created a system in which the potential to evolve into perfection can occur. This system is the reincarnation cycle. We won't go over the principles of reincarnation again because we covered them in a prior chapter.

We've all heard the adage "nobody's perfect." Every lie that contains a smidgeon of truth is readily accepted by the unthinking mind, and this cliche is a lie wrought by the serpentine mind of the fallen angels, mankind's adversary—to stall, retard, and prevent man's reintegration with his Source; to immobilize his spiritual movement upward in the evolutionary spiral.

The repetition of such "heinous" terms operates as a suggestion to men's subconscious levels, convincing them that such a goal whose mark was set by Life, by God, is unattainable by man. We must remove ourselves from such a false notion, for believing in it means ceasing to think, act, and speak righteously and gloriously.

Human perfection, in the sense of displaying divine attributes, is attainable, and there are men and women who have attained it. They are destiny's lords, and the basic difference between them and immature human souls is their own vibratory rate, their soul-frequency—the frequency of consciousness and its expressions.

Though perfection is relative, man can achieve human perfection—this is godhood—and this is only an imperfect level of godliness on the scale of divinity.

Personal labor, ego-effacement, and SELF-placement are used to eventually achieve perfection. One of Origen's significant beliefs was the attainment of perfection in stages rather than on a certain day of resurrection at the last trumpet call.

 Thomas Kempis, another writer on Christian ideas, stated in his literary work "the Imitation of Christ" that,

"If every year we rooted out one vice, we should soon become perfect man."

Christhood is the universal destiny of all children of the light. True Christians are those who demonstrate Christ in their everyday life; this is true adoration. This is the "Second-Coming" of the Gnostics, those who interpret the Nazarene Master's precepts in an esoteric manner. The Christ savior is man's reality, his Real Self, his cosmic blueprint, which he will eventually out-picture in his waking consciousness, not in some distant future in heavenly worlds, but right now and now. Everything that is expected to be accomplished in Heaven in the afterlife must be accomplished now.

St. Paul grasped this knowledge and passed it on to others who were ready and willing to receive it. He stated that the Christ within us is our *"hope and glory" (Col 1:27)* and that we should shape this Son of God within us (Gal 4:19).

Jesus, the man, became the Christ and therefore demonstrated the path, the means by which Christhood is accomplished.

"I AM the Way, the Truth, and the Life," Jesus declared (John 14:6), signifying his function as an exemplar, a model to which we should aspire in order to obtain our own Christhood, our own Sonship of the Godhead.

It follows that we attain salvation not by believing, in relying on another being to save us from our own human faults, weaknesses, and sins, but by replacing our human-ness with the virtues of our own Christ Reality through our own personal effort in manifesting Christ in our daily consciousness, by eliminating the sense of a false ego, "the beast that was, and is not, and yet is" (Rev 17:11,18). This work contains a lot of repetition because our paper is meant to stir up the sleeping soul.

As the roots of all vices, the false ego and ignorance conceal the individual's divinity. Spirituality is the identification and manifestation of man's true Self; this also includes the Self's non-identifying with the flesh, emotions, and cognition. This is the first and, ironically, the last crucial step that the aspirant must take on the Path of Ascension.

It is critical to awaken the heart, to cultivate bodhicitta, or compassion, and to become aware of the true essence of things. Love is believed to be blind. This is an incorrect assumption. Love is super-sighted, whilst lust is blind.

Man's consciousness and senses expand to comprehend the other manifestations of Nature when enthralled by Love. The lower self should be decentralized and effaced. The greater life is achieved by not adhering to the false ego.

A man who lives solely for sensuous pleasures is a man who has died. St. Paul expresses it this way:

" . . . to be carnally minded is death; but to be spiritually minded is life and peace." (Romans 8:6)

Whatever religion, sect, or belief system we follow or do not follow, the work of obtaining perfection is plainly before us. The Omniversal Collective does not profit from poor reintegration with the Father. We were born in this state, and we must bravely return to be something more.

If the belief that one is "saved" simply by believing in a savior were real, then flawed individuals would find their way to Heaven— these men would quickly convert Paradise into a living Hell due to their vices and bad expressions.
Death, nor mere beliefs or faith, can change a person into an angel of Light. Where we shall be in the cosmic scheme of things is determined by our own level of consciousness.

When one's will is aligned with God's will, when one's consciousness is one with God's consciousness, one is liberated from mortal constraints and finitude. This mystical state was the consciousness-level attained by Saints and Sages throughout history.

For example, Enoch walked with God and subsequently lost his identity in the Light of his divinity; his ego was "not," displaced by the expression of his real spiritual SELF (Gen 5:24).

What one man has done, another man can do; all that is necessary is sincerity, perseverance, effort, discipline, and practice—"practice makes perfect," as the saying goes.

The Christ life comes before the union of our soul with the Godhead. The virtues of Christ should be expressed in our daily lives. They are like beads that we string together and adorn ourselves with. Only beings who have attained perfection are permitted to live in God's kingdom.

To emphasize our point, if spiritually immature people were let into the "Kingdom of God," they would turn the place upside down, resulting in pandemonium. The universe is ordered, especially in the celestial spheres; even primeval chaos is ordered when viewed from divine viewpoints.

The fact that only perfection exists in God's kingdom should cause us to reevaluate Jesus' message: did he urge us to worship him, or did he teach us to copy his life, his manner of life, and thus become perfect? When considering natural laws and cross-referencing with other religions, the answer should be apparent enough.

We are most likely to achieve the objective of human life if we acquire a virtue at a time. The slothful wait for deliverance from someone else, but the wise are captains of their souls, and they take charge of the helm of life by giving their Christ presence full control of their ship sailing through the turbulent, and sometimes tranquil, sea of life.

The events in Jesus' life are the story of every soul who visits the physical world. Each person will experience the transfiguration, the crucifixion, the resurrection, and the ascension—all of which are tied to various initiations bestowed by Life—at some point in their lives.

To be spiritual, to be holy, one must have a constant awareness of one's inherent divinity. Our thinking, doing, and speaking should all be spiritual in nature. The Piscean avatar proclaims in the Gospel of Thomas:

"If you will not fast from the world, you will not find the kingdom."

From another literary source, the Pistis Sophia, we find this same precept expressed a little differently:

". . . renounce the world and the whole matter therein."

To be more specific, we should live in the world yet not be a part of it; to live as a renunciate in the midst of life's ups and downs; or, in other words, to live as a karma yogi. We honor and worship the Great One by living the Christ life, whether you call it Tao, Allah, Parabrahm, the Absolute, I AM Presence, or whatever you want; terminology will not change Truth, because Truth is immutable; however, it may cause schisms and bigotry in the minds of immature souls who are unable to see beyond the form, beyond the letter of the law, and into the Spirit. Unity should be recognized amid apparent diversity because Oneness is Reality and diversity is an illusion.

Life is directing us toward perfection. It provides us with opportunities to grow, unfold, and materialize the blueprint of our reality, the God-Image that was so lovingly bestowed upon us. Let us not believe that human perfection is the ultimate objective, for even if a creature is humanly perfect, he is still an imperfect god. There will always be higher heights to climb.

The succeeding battle and strivings to be a flawless god are simply another stage, another cosmic phase of work that will eventually allow us to govern over even greater things that the human mind is still unable to fathom. Evolution is the law that governs man's progress, and it is a smart person who walks with the flow rather than against it.

Please keep in mind that when we talk about evolution, we're talking about the soul or awareness part of the microcosm, not the physical form itself.

Conquering matter's and the carnal mind's resistance is not without suffering and, strangely, joy; but the serious alchemist who seeks to convert his being into God's glorious manifestation will soon detect the so-called sacrifices that he makes from a spiritual standpoint.

Sacrifices shall be regarded as sacraments offered to the Godhead, and they will be offered with divine reverence and love. Earthly voices will no longer dissuade him from obeying his Holy Christ Self. People sometimes perceive such a person who is close to and united with God and his higher spiritual parts as insane.

The mystical achievement and sacredness of the spiritual initiate—the kingdom's little ones—will never be comprehended by mass consciousness. Such a person would be stoned.

"Take heed that ye despise not one of these little ones; for I say unto you, That in heaven their angels do always behold the face of my Father which is in heaven." (Matt18:10)

Life is short and unpredictable. It's a shame to leave this physical plane without knowing the meaning of life or one's true identity. Going to the beyond through the change of death does not transform us into something we are not, it does not expand our consciousness, and it does not naturally unfold the light within us; it is an orthodox Christian fallacy to maintain that by going to churches or temples, or professing one's faith in this or that savior, or dogma, one would earn a place in the celestial realms, that one would automatically be perfect on the day of reckoning; and this phi This is Churchianity at its worst: the display of primitive logic and maudlin emotionalism in relation to their beliefs' false sense of superiority.

Orthodox Christianity is not the only religion with this mindset; it may be seen among adherents of any religious system. As previously stated, perfection demands effort and our own participation.

Allow others to do the work, and we will be brainwashed into believing that the globe is flat and that it was created in 4004 BC; we will be mobilized and coerced to kill and torture in the name of Religion, Love, and God. There is enough proof of this throughout history.

Salvation

Exoteric Christians call "salvation" the avoidance of eternal damnation in a burning fire called "Hell." For some, being in Hell without God is preferable to being in Heaven with His presence.

From an esoteric standpoint, the belief in Hell as a place created by God is nonsensical. Hell is a state of mind, a state of consciousness, a disposition, and an attitude, much like heaven.

Every aggregate, every matter expression, every occurrence is in the process of becoming. Because there is no permanence in Nature, it is impossible for a place like a "lake of fire" to persist indefinitely.
The compassionate Father would not build such a horror and exile his children there "forever and ever." God does not punish but consumes that which is humble inside man in order for him to be acceptable in the eyes of the Spirit.

Creations are transient; emanations of God are, in a sense, eternal, even if they exist in cycles of Activity and Rest. It is heresy to believe that a God of Love would construct Hell to punish wrongdoers for all eternity. The devil-mind views God as a terrifying, wrathful being who eagerly sends sinful men into a blazing ring for His own divine delight. The devil-mind opposes the children of Light approaching the Divine Throne and becoming one with the Supreme Being. This will be avoided at all costs.

A flawed theology is to blame for the spread of the idea that man, by nature, is a sinful being. To achieve the condition known as salvation, we are taught to believe that the instrument of spiritual survival is faith in another, in a man whom they see as the unique son of God—which is just a mask for what they truly want us to believe.

The truth, as we see it, is that the clergy, with their egoistic nature, wants the poor man on the street to see them and their institution as a weapon of salvation and as God's intermediaries, rather than on self-reliance. This belief is deceptive. It leads man down roads that lead nowhere, leaving him lost in a labyrinth of delusion.

Man must learn to be his own High Priest, with no one to intervene between him and God. This is how Nature wants it; it is what God and the higher intelligences; the celestial hierarchies want man to understand. The Christ inside is the "single" son of God, the profound mystery instilled in pupils by the Gurus of the Esoteric Christian tradition.

Exercises involving the summoned presence and the development of divinity are used in

Christian mysticism to help the Christ child within grow. Some examples are as follows:

- Constantly reflecting on the knowledge of God's presence, both within and without.

- Constantly reflecting on God's nature and attributes.

- Visualizing and nourishing God's triple flame within the heart on a daily basis.

- Manifesting the traits and nature of God in daily life.

- Invoking God's focused presence in one's consciousness (the Shekinah).

- Constantly listening to the "still, little voice," the "Voice of Silence," the Supreme Word resonating.

- Increasing the Light quotient in the microcosm's lower force-field through visualization, prayers, and invocations.

- Concentrating on the spiritual star of initiation until it forms a protective halo around one's head.

- Sessions of attunement with the Higher Christ Self.

- Force conservation, sublimation, and transformation.

- Meditation and mystical recitations are practiced.

The Gnostic View of Salvation

According to the exoteric Church, people who believe in the man Jesus will experience the physical resurrection of their decaying body or bones on the day of reckoning. We would all inherit, or rather enter, God's kingdom if we obeyed and believed the dogmas devised by the priesthood.

It is unfortunate that man believes in such fantastical concepts, especially since St. Paul himself declares:

"flesh and blood cannot inherit the kingdom of God, nor does the perishable inherit the imperishable." (I Cor 15:50)

With the preceding verse as a model for Truth, one is struck by Tertullian's (around 190 AD) clear opinion that anyone who opposes the resurrection of the flesh is a heretic. Even in the early days of Christianity, falsehoods and deceptions seeped into the Church, which the Christ Master (whom we should all honor and respect) repudiated and denounced as satanic ideas.

The true secret of resurrection, of etherealization of the physical form, was passed down in secret and silently to a select few who were worthy, those who could "handle" the sacred science.

From an esoteric perspective, salvation is analogous to what Hindu philosophy refers to as "moksha," "mukti," "kaivalya," or the more familiar occidental phrase, "Liberation"— liberation from the cycle of birth and rebirth, or reincarnation, and ignorance. Buddhists consider redemption to be the attainment of Nirvana, or the "blowing-out" of the false ego, which results in liberation from one's sojourn in the lower domains. An Arhat, or "Child of God," is someone who has attained such a state.

Truth, according to the Piscean avatar, will set us free. What exactly is this freedom? We are all familiar with social and political liberties such as freedom of expression, freedom of worship, freedom to assemble, and freedom of the press. There are certain esoteric liberties that our devotions to and application of Truth would reveal to us, such as:

- Freedom from past karma; liberation from ignorance and carnal impulses that generate new karma.

- The absence of pain, sorrow, deterioration, and death.

- Freedom from the five senses' constraints.

- Freedom from physical constraints.

- Self-ignorance, fear, and superstition are all gone.

- The ability to obtain knowledge and wisdom straight from God.

- The ability to worship the Almighty directly in our own unique way.

- God's gift to man is liberty. It is man's right to claim it. The essence of true freedom can be expressed as the ability to mirror God's image, as we were meant to do.

Masonry's ceremonies with the Cable Tow represent mortal constraints. The severance of the Cable allows man to work for the Master in the higher worlds. In a spiritual sense, freedom signifies man's ability to receive holy communion from the Monad, his "Father in Heaven."

This is depicted in Genesis' parable of the three characters: Lot, Abraham, and Melchizedek. According to one portion of the story, Lots represents the human consciousness, which is held captive by wicked rulers embodying carnal thoughts and lower urges of animal instincts.

Abraham, or the Higher Self, comes to the rescue and offers tithes in the form of spiritual nourishment—transmuted energies—to Melchizedek, who personifies the Monad, the Divine Spark inside man, as a mediator between the higher and lower. Melchizedek, for his part, offers Abraham his spiritual force and substance in the form of bread and wine.

To summarize, this is the esoteric reality of Holy Communion, the Eucharist, as it occurs in the microcosm.

Let us conclude this topic with a short New Testament phrase that captures our theme of redemption via human effort throughout these pages:

"... work out your own salvation with fear and trembling." (Phil 2:12)

The Esoteric Concept of God

Certain sects of Orthodox Christianity have unusual ideas about God: he is thought to have human form (since God created man in his image), a threefold personality, and a strong male predominance; Christians believe he resides somewhere in heaven or perhaps the clouds.

Apart from being the son, Jesus is also thought to be one and the same as the ultimate God, despite his own declaration that he is not the Absolute:

" ... Verily, verily, I say unto you, The Son can do nothing of himself, but what he seeth the Father do: for what things soever he doeth, these also doeth the Son likewise. (John:5:19)

" ... My God, my God, why hast thou forsaken me?" (Mark15:34)

Regarding the nature of God, the Old Testament, when taken literally, is quite shocking to spiritual sensibilities.

Essentially God is a liar for he told Adam and Eve that they would die after eating the fruit of the Tree of Knowledge which did not subsequently occur after their indigestion of the fruit:

"But of the tree of the knowledge of good and evil, thou shalt not eat of it: for in the day that thou eatest thereof thou shalt surely die." *(Gen:2:17)*

God is a deceiver since he told Moses that his name, Jehovah, was unknown to Abraham, yet the Patriarch named a place Jehovah-jireh to honor Him:

"And I appeared unto Abraham, unto Isaac, and unto Jacob, by the name of God Almighty, but by my name JEHOVAH was I not known to them." (Ex 6:3) "And Abraham called the name of that place Jehovah-jireh: as it is said to this day, In the mount of the LORD it shall be seen." (Gen 22:14)

God has human flaws and shortcomings. He is described as a tyrant who punishes those who oppose him; he is portrayed as a jealous God and a megalomaniac who needs our devotion to satisfy his ego:

"Thou shalt not bow down thyself to them, nor serve them: for I the LORD thy God am a jealous God, visiting the iniquity of the fathers upon the children unto the third and fourth generation of them that hate me." (Ex 20:5)

"For thou shalt worship no other god: for the LORD, whose name is Jealous, is a jealous God." (Ex 34:14)

God is confused at times and not omniscient or all-knowing:

"And the LORD said, Shall I hide from Abraham that thing which I do." (Gen18:17)

*"And the LORD God called unto Adam, and
said unto him, Where art thou?" (Gen 3:9)
"And he said, Who told thee that thou wast
naked? Hast thou eaten of the tree, whereof I
commanded thee that thou shouldest not eat?"
(Gen:3:11)*

*"And the LORD said unto Cain, Where is
Abel thy brother?" (Gen:4:9).*

God is likewise prone to outbursts of rage
and wrath:

*"And the LORD rooted them out of their
land in anger, and in wrath, and in great
indignation, and cast them into another land,
as it is this day." (Deu:29:28)*

*"Notwithstanding the LORD turned not
from the fierceness of his great wrath,
wherewith his anger was kindled against
Judah, because of all the provocations that
Manasseh had provoked him withal." (2 Kings
23:26)*

*God is also partial and given to favoritism:
" . . . saith the LORD: yet I loved Jacob, and I
hated Esau, and laid his mountains and his
heritage waste for the dragons of the
wilderness." (Mal1:2,3)*

There are many more unpleasant depictions
of God—the examples above should get you
thinking. It is comforting to know, however,
that these portrayals of God are not to be taken
literally and have a deeper, symbolic
significance. According to at least one Rabbi,
the more discrepancies we find in the Torah
and Talmud, the more profound and symbolic
their meaning becomes.

The true esoteric understanding of God is not explicitly written in the scriptures. Jehovah or Yahweh is not the Absolute God recognized by Jesus, and certainly not as his "Father." The genuine teachings on this subject can be discovered in the Qabalah, the Rabbis' secret, mystical oral heritage.

Esoteric Christians understand that God is Light, Life, and Love; that God is both immanent and transcendent in his manifestations.

Those who possess the gnosis understand that God is omniscient, almighty, and omnipresent, and that nothing can limit or restrict the Source.

The Supreme Being is the Uncreated, the Unborn, and the Unformed. God is not anyplace, but "everything" is within the One's infinite being.

This is the circle whose circumference is everywhere but whose center is nowhere; or whose circumference is everywhere but whose center is nowhere.

This is the Almighty, infinite and eternal, ever-existent, ever-conscious, ever-blissful, whom no language can adequately express, or the intellect fully comprehend.

Conclusion

There are many mysteries in the Bible, and even more mysteries in life that are not addressed in the Holy Scriptures.

When one attains a spiritual awareness, more of the true content of the Bible is revealed—this is the esoteric side of the Bible that the child of God would grab in his consciousness and make as jewels in the Kingdom of God within his own consciousness.

May everybody who reads this text aspire to attain this mystical consciousness and delve into the deeper meanings reserved for the few—the few are not selected; they choose to be chosen.

Made in United States
Troutdale, OR
04/29/2024

19539237R00056